The Magician's Nephew

A Play

C. S. Lewis and Glyn Robbins

A SAMUEL FRENCH ACTING EDITION

SAMUEL
FRENCH
FOUNDED 1830

SAMUELFRENCH-LONDON.CO.UK
SAMUELFRENCH.COM

FOR AMATEUR PRODUCTION ENQUIRIES

UNITED KINGDOM AND WORLD
EXCLUDING NORTH AMERICA
plays@SamuelFrench-London.co.uk
020 7255 4302/01

Each title is subject to availability from Samuel French,

depending upon country of performance.

THE MAGICIAN'S NEPHEW

Presented by Vanessa Ford Productions Ltd in association with Aldersgate Productions Ltd, Theatre Royal Presentations plc and Westminster Productions Ltd at the Ashcroft Theatre, Croydon on September 20th, 1988, and subsequently on tour and at the Westminster Theatre, London, with the following cast of characters:

Digory Kirke	Kieron Smith
Polly Plummer	Antonia Loyd
Uncle Andrew	John Hester
Jadis, Queen of Queens	Elizabeth Elvin
Aunt Letitia	Judith Carpenter
Strawberry	Tom Skippings
The Fat Man	James Mathews
Policeman	Robert Neil Kingham
Errand Boys	Craig Almond
	Sean Arberry
Cabby	John Talbot
The Man with a Meerschaum	Mark Hayford
The Soldier	Mark Hayford
Aslan	Robert Neil Kingham
Beaver	Craig Almond
Rabbit	Sean Arberry
Bulldog	Mark Hayford
Jackdaw	James Mathews
Owl	Judith Carpenter
Nellie	Pippa Lay
Fledge	Tom Skippings
Mrs Kirke (Mother)	Pippa Lay

The play directed by Richard Williams

The play takes place in Victorian London at the turn of this century; in the Wood Between the Worlds; in the Ruined City of Charn; in various parts of the World of Narnia.

CHARACTERS

Polly
Digory
Uncle Andrew
Jadis, a Witch
Aunt Letitia
Strawberry (later called Fledge), a Horse
Fat Man
Cabby (later King Frank of Narnia)
Policeman 1
Man in deerstalker hat
Errand Boy
Policeman 2
Soldier
Aslan, the Lion
Rabbit
Jackdaw
Bulldog
Owl
Beaver
Nellie (later Queen Helen of Narnia)
Mother

Assorted citizens of Charn and of Narnia

SYNOPSIS OF SCENES

Please note that the following billing should be used on all programmes and posters connected with performances of this play:

The Magician's Nephew

by

C. S. Lewis

Adapted by Glyn Robbins

COVER ILLUSTRATION

The cover illustration for this play is reproduced by kind permission of the artist, Charles Jamieson, whose copyright it remains. Enquiries regarding the use of it, for whatever purpose, must be addressed to the artist c/o The Editorial Department, Samuel French Ltd.

SOME BACKGROUND TO THE PLAY

There were once four children who had a remarkable adventure while staying with a Professor Kirke, when they opened the door of a seemingly ordinary wardrobe made of apple-wood and found themselves in a quite different world from ours called Narnia. There they helped the rightful ruler of that land, the magnificent Great Lion, Aslan, to fight and conquer the Wicked White Witch, who had put a spell on Narnia and turned the land to ice and snow. That story is told in the book and the play *The Lion, The Witch and The Wardrobe*. For a time those children became Kings and Queens of Narnia and seemed to rule for years and years. But when they eventually did come back to our world, they found no-one had noticed their being away, because our time and Narnian time is very, very different.

Today, we go back to the beginning. We will meet Digory Kirke and Polly Plummer, two young people who live next door to each other in London at the turn of this century. Digory and his mother (who is ill) are staying with relations because Digory's father is away working in India. Digory's Uncle Andrew thinks of himself as a great magician. Aunt Letitia, his sister, doesn't. We will find out who is right and what happens when magic spells don't quite behave as expected. We will also see why Aslan is the rightful ruler of the land of Narnia; who the people of that country are; who is in charge of them; and how wickedness came first to London and then got taken to Narnia.

G.R.

Other Narnian plays adapted by Glyn Robbins from novels by C. S. Lewis and which are available in French's Acting Editions are:

The Lion, The Witch and The Wardrobe
The Voyage of The Dawn Treader

ACT I

Edwardian London. A cold, wet summer evening

The Curtain *rises on an attic room in a late Victorian London terraced house. The room is furnished as a sitting-room and filled with bookshelves. A high-backed armchair with its back to us (in which Uncle Andrew is secreted) faces a flickering coal fire. There is a table covered in books, ledgers, ink-bottles, pens and a microscope. Also on the table is a bright red wooden tray with yellow and green rings on it, and a pair of black leather gauntlets. We become aware of the gentle hiss of gas-lighting, of the ticking of a clock, of a soft strange humming noise, like an old-fashioned vacuum cleaner being used a long way away*

A hidden door opens slowly and a girl, Polly, and a boy, Digory, climb furtively into the room

Polly It's all right Digory. There's no one here.

Digory This is no good, Polly. No good at all. You said the house next door was completely deserted and empty. Look around. This place isn't empty. It's full of things. Thank goodness, there's nobody here. We'd better go back before someone comes. If we get caught like this, they'll think we're burglars or something.

Polly Are you scared?

Digory Of course not. But if your father was far away in India, and your mother was very ill, and you had to live with a fierce aunt and an uncle who's a mad inventor ... and if the real reason they were looking after you was that your mother was going to—going to die, well, you wouldn't want to get caught, would you? By anyone. Doing anything.

Polly I suppose not. Is your uncle really mad?

Digory Well, he's either mad, or there's some real mystery about him. He's got a room with a door that's always locked. And Aunt Letitia says I must never go up there.

Polly That's strange. I wonder why? What's she like?

Digory Who? Aunt Letitia? She's really fierce, and a bit strange. Uncle Andrew's afraid of her, I think. Whenever he tries to say anything to me at meal times, she always shuts him up. She tells him: "Don't worry the boy" or "I'm sure Digory doesn't want to hear about that," or she tells me to go and play in the garden. As though she doesn't want us to talk together at all.

Polly What sort of things does he try to say?

Digory I don't know. He never gets far enough.

Polly So your uncle's got a room that he locks up, and your aunt won't let him talk to you. Digory, that's not being mad—that's just grown-ups.

Digory It's more than that, Polly. Last night, when I was going past the stairs that lead up to his locked door, I'm sure I heard a scream.

Polly A scream? Perhaps he keeps a wife up there in leg-irons and chained to the wall. And he's starving her to death so he can inherit all her fortune.

Digory I wondered about that. He's never got any money. He's always borrowing from Aunt Letitia. But the scream wasn't a human one.

Polly Really, and then what?

Digory Well, I ran into my room and turned out the light. And jumped into bed and hid under the bedclothes, of course. Then I heard him. Uncle Andrew. Creeping down the stairs and along the hall and into my bedroom. And then he kind of slithered across the carpet. And tore back the bedclothes and stared at me with those awful eyes of his.

Polly Then what? Then what?

Digory Then he said, in a terrible voice, "Boy! Were you spying on me?"

Polly What did you say?

Digory I said, "No, Uncle Andrew, I was just going to bed."

Polly And then?

Digory Then he said, still staring really hard at me, "Never spy on me, Digory, or something dreadful will happen to you." Then he slithered out of the room again.

Polly All in the dark?

Digory Yes, all in the dark.

Polly How horrid!

Digory So that's why I think he's mad. But anyway, this place is no good for a real adventure. It's not empty and either we've explored the roof too far or we haven't explored far enough. Either way, it means your measurements were all wrong.

Polly I can't help it. You did the sums, too.

Digory I told you I'm not good at arithmetic.

Polly Well, neither am I.

Digory That's pretty obvious. Let's go back.

Polly Why don't we go on?

Digory Because it's nearly six o'clock, and by the time we get back and get washed and cleaned up, it'll be dinner time.

Polly Oh, all right. But let's have a look around here first. (*Pointing*) What do you think those are?

Digory Those? They look like yellow and green—

Suddenly the high-backed chair spins round to reveal Uncle Andrew. He is tall, very thin; with a clean-shaven face, sharply pointed nose; bright eyes; and a clouded mop of grey hair

Digory }
Polly } (*together*) Aaah!

Digory Uncle Andrew! We've got into your room, by mistake.

Uncle Andrew Surprise, surprise! Got here by mistake, eh? And two of you, as well.

Polly makes for the door

Don't try to run away, little girl. I always lock the door. Two children are exactly what I wanted. Who's this, Digory?

Polly Please Mr Ketterley, I'm Polly from next door and it's nearly my dinner time, and I've got to go home. Will you let us out please? Right now.

Uncle Andrew Not just yet, Polly-from-next-door. This is far too good an opportunity. I wanted two children. For my work. You see, I'm in the middle of a most important experiment.

Polly Digory, say something.

Digory Look here, Uncle Andrew ...

Uncle Andrew A most important experiment. It seemed to work all right on a guinea-pig last night. But then a guinea-pig can't talk and tell you things. And you can't tell a guinea-pig how to come back.

Polly Digory! That was the scream you heard. A guinea-pig. Say something.

Digory Uncle Andrew, it's nearly six o'clock, and dinner time. And Polly's father will be looking for her. And Aunt Letty will be looking for me. And she'll be looking for you too, Uncle.

Polly If you really did need us for your experiment thing, we could always come back after dinner.

Uncle Andrew Ah, but how do I know you *would* come back? Dinner time, eh? Aunt Letty looking for us. Polly's father. Mmmmmm ... (*He seems to change his mood*) Well, well, if you really must go, I suppose you must. I can't really expect two youngsters like you to understand how lonely I am, sometimes. Working here all by myself. The weight of the world is on my shoulders. Pity the poor Magician. Ours is a high and lonely destiny. But then how could you understand, children? No matter. Go to your dinner, Polly-from-next-door. I ought to give you a present before you go. After all, it's not every day that sees a little girl in my dingy old study—especially such a very attractive young lady as you, Polly.

Polly Why thank you, Mr Ketterley.

Uncle Andrew Just call me Uncle Andrew, my dear. Now about this present. Would you like one of my rings?

Digory He's up to something. Look at his face.

Polly I think he's quite nice, really. Oh yes, please, Uncle Andrew, I would like one. One of those green ones, please.

Uncle Andrew Not a green one, Polly dear. I can't give the green ones away, today. But you can certainly have a yellow one. Here, try this one on.

Polly Yes, I will.

Digory Polly, don't be a fool!

A loud humming noise begins

Polly What's that humming sound?

Digory Don't touch the ring—

Polly It's getting louder.

Digory Get rid of it. It's terrible danger!

Polly It's as though the rings were making it.

Polly disappears

Digory (*shouting*) Polly, where are you? Polly! Polly!

Uncle Andrew (*holding Digory*) None of that. If you shout any louder, your poor, sick mother will hear. And you know what that'll do to her. There (*He releases Digory*) That's better. Perhaps you couldn't help it. It is a shock when you see someone vanish. It gave *me* a good turn when the guinea-pig did it the other night, I can tell you.

Digory What happened to Polly?

Uncle Andrew Congratulate me, dear boy. My experiment has succeeded. Polly-from-next-door has gone—vanished—right out of this world.

Digory What have you done to her?

Uncle Andrew Sent her to another place. To another world.

Digory What *do* you mean?

Uncle Andrew The yellow rings are made from the dust of another world, brought here when our world was only just beginning. The rings draw you back to that other world. By magic. I wanted to find out what that world was really like.

Digory Well, why didn't you go yourself, then?

Uncle Andrew Me? *ME*? Are you mad? A man at my time of life, in my state of health, to risk the shock of being thrown into another world, into another universe?! Why, you might meet up with *anything*.

Digory So you sent Polly in your place. Even if you are my uncle, you've behaved like a coward.

Uncle Andrew BE SILENT! I will not be talked to like that! I am the great scholar, the Master Magician. I am in charge of the experiment. Of course I could not go. You don't send generals to fight battles, you send soldiers. So I sent guinea-pigs first, and now I've sent Polly.

Digory And how are you going to bring her back?

Uncle Andrew The yellow rings draw you to the other world. The green ones draw you back to our world.

Digory But you wouldn't let Polly have a green ring.

Uncle Andrew Quite right.

Digory So she can't get back!

Uncle Andrew Oh, but she can get back. If, that is, *someone* in this room were brave enough and honourable enough to go to the aid of a lady in distress . . . If that someone went after her wearing a yellow ring himself and taking two green ones with him, then she could get back.

Digory And that someone couldn't possibly be you, could it? Well, of course I'll go and help Polly. She's my friend.

Uncle Andrew Excellent, excellent. Now here's what to do. (*He puts on the gloves*) The rings only work if they're actually touching your skin. Wearing gloves like this, I can pick them up and nothing happens. The moment you touch a yellow ring you vanish out of this world. And my theory is that the moment you touch a green ring you vanish from the other world and reappear in this one. Now, I'm picking up these two green rings, one for you and one for Polly, and dropping them in your right-hand pocket. (*He does so*) Now, you must pick up a yellow one for yourself. Put it on your finger, there'll be less chance then of losing it.

Digory (*going to pick up the ring*) But what about my mother? If she wakes up and I'm not there, she'll get worried and make herself really ill again.

Uncle Andrew Getting scared, are we? Oh, well, just as you please. Go down to your darling Mummy, and have your dinner. Leave your little friend Polly to be eaten up by wild animals or to drown or starve or be lost for good in the Other World. I don't care. It's all one to me. Be a little coward.

Digory If I were big enough, I'd punch your head.

Digory picks up the ring. As he does so, the loud humming noise begins again. He takes a deep breath and closes his eyes

Well, here we go.

Uncle Andrew The sooner you go, the sooner you'll be back. (*He laughs*)

The humming noise gets very much louder; the room fills with haze and green light; Uncle Andrew's laugh becomes evil and echoes

The room and Uncle Andrew vanish

Leaving Digory in:

SCENE 2

The Wood Between the Worlds

Polly is lying asleep on the ground

Digory (*opening his eyes*) Well, that was really strange! Like swimming under water—except I'm dry all over. And what a strange place this is; all these trees and pools of water. It's so quiet, too. No birds singing; no insects humming; no wind blowing. You can almost feel the trees growing. It feels sort of rich, like plumcake or Christmas pudding. (*He sees Polly*) Polly! Polly! Wake up!

Polly (*waking*) Oh hello, boy. Haven't I seen you somewhere before?

Digory Of course you have, Polly. You live next door. You're my best friend. Don't you remember? Crawling over the rafters into Uncle Andrew's room? Finding the rings?

Polly It sounds familiar. Like a dream.

Digory Polly, it's me, Digory.

Polly Yes, yes, Digory. Of course. What rings?

Digory Look! Over there!

Polly Why it's a guinea-pig, nosing about in the grass. But what's that strapped to its back?

Digory It's a ring. A bright yellow ring. And you've got one just like it on your finger. And so have I.

Polly Of course. Your Uncle Andrew gave it to me. And then things went funny.

Digory He was experimenting. Using us as his next guinea-pigs. The horrible man still is.

Polly What do we do now? Take the guinea-pig and go back?

Digory (*yawning*) There's no real hurry!

Polly I think there is. The place is too quiet. Too dreamy. You're yawning; and I feel very sleepy. If we're not careful we might lie down and sleep for ever. We've got to go back. Right now.

Digory The guinea-pig looks so happy here. Let's leave him. Uncle Andrew will only do something horrid to him.

Polly Right, now. How do we get back?

Digory We go back to the pool and jump in.

Polly It looks very deep. And we aren't dressed for swimming.

Digory We don't need to be. Remember, we didn't get wet on the way here. Come on, let's jump.

Polly Can you swim?

Digory A bit. Can you?

Polly Not much.

Digory Well, hold my hand. Shut your eyes. Now. One—two—three—go!

They jump into the pool. Nothing happens

Polly Nothing's happened. What's wrong?

They get out of the pool

Digory I must have forgotten something.

Polly What?

Digory Oh, I know. Of course. We're still wearing our yellow rings. They're the ones that got us here. We need to change them for green ones to take us back. Have you got two pockets? Put the yellow ring into the left-hand one. Now put this green one on your finger and we'll try again.

Polly does as he instructs

Ready. Shut your eyes. One—two—three—hold it!

Polly What now, Digory?

Digory I've had a wonderful idea. If this pool leads to our world, won't all the other pools lead to lots of other worlds?

Polly You mean this wood might be only one of them?

Digory I think this wood is a sort of in-between place for all of the worlds. Like the tunnel in the rafters in the attic at home. With all kinds of different worlds leading off of it. And once you've got to the in-between place, you can go anywhere.

Polly Well, even if you can ...

Digory And that explains why it's so quiet and sleepy here. Nothing ever happens. Just like at home, in the in-between places between the walls and above the ceiling or under the floors. Hey, this is exciting.

Polly The Wood Between The Worlds.

Digory Come on. Let's have a real adventure. Let's try another pool. (*Pointing*) Let's try that one.

Polly Digory! Wait!

Digory Oh, come on, Polly!

Polly You must wait! How will we know which is our pool? Our way back? They all look the same. We must mark our one.

Digory Oh, crikey. That was close!

Polly It's a good thing one of us has some common sense.

Digory I'll kick a mark in the grass, here. (*Kicking*) Like this.

Polly Bigger! That's better. Sometimes boys really are stupid!

Digory And so are girls, sometimes.

Polly Oh, no they're not.

Digory Come on, girl. Don't keep gassing on about it! I want to see what's in another pool.

Polly All right then. But I'm not holding hands.

Digory Suit yourself. Let's try this pool. Got your green ring on? Ready? One—two—three, jump.

Darkness. The rushing sound of a great wind. Whirling lights, whirling shapes. A red glow. And as the light settles down, we find ourselves in:

SCENE 3

The Hall of Queens

The Hall's features include a square pillar about four foot high topped with an arch from which is suspended a bell; a hammer rests nearby. There is a row of perfectly still, beautifully dressed figures wearing crowns nearby. One of these is Jadis. There are also two great doors and a glassless window through which comes the redness of the setting sun against a black sky

Digory What a weird place!

Polly I don't like it. It makes me shiver.

Digory What a very strange light. There's no movement in it. There's no life to it.

Polly And where does it come from? The sky is black.

Digory Perhaps we're in for a thunderstorm or an eclipse or something. Do you think anyone lives here?

Polly They can't. It's all in ruins. There hasn't been a sound since we got here. Listen!

Pause. Silence

Let's go home, I don't like it . . .

Digory Let's look around a bit. There's those waxworks over there. They look interesting. What wonderful clothes.

Polly I wonder why they haven't rotted away long ago. The materials are lovely—just like new. There must be something in the air that keeps them fresh.

Digory It's magic.

Polly What is?

Digory It's magic that keeps them fresh. There's a spell on this room.

Polly You don't believe in magic, do you? Spells and witches and things? That's all stuff and nonesense.

Digory Well how do you think we got here? Which reminds me, take your green ring off—

Polly does so

—and put it in your right-hand pocket. Have you still got your yellow ring in your left pocket?

Polly nods

Good. These all look like very nice people.
Polly Except for this one.
Digory She's the most beautiful woman I've ever seen.
Polly I can't see anything special in her. Come on, let's go.
Digory Let's just look at that bell thing.
Polly Oh come on, Digory, I'm hungry.
Digory Just one look. There's some writing on the pillar.
Polly It's hiero—hierothingies—you can't read them.
Digory I can't, but I sort of can, if you know what I mean.

> "Make your choice, adventurous stranger,
> Strike the bell and bide the danger,
> Or wonder, till it drives you mad,
> What would have followed, if you had."

Polly Danger? Danger? Come on, let's go.
Digory If we do go, we'll wonder what would have followed for the rest of our lives.
Polly That's fine by me.
Digory Well, it isn't by me.

Digory grabs the hammer and strikes the bell. It makes a sweet sound

Polly You beast!
Digory You—you girl!

They start to fight. The sweet note of the bell gets louder and louder and more menacing, turning into the great crashing sound of falling masonry. The children cower together now, clutching each other. The sound stops

Polly There, I hope you're satisfied now.
Digory Thank goodness that's all over!

From amongst the figures, one, Jadis, stirs

Jadis Who has awakened me? Who has broken the spell?
Digory I think it must have been me.
Jadis You? You? But you are only a child—a common child. Anyone can see that you have not one drop of noble blood in your veins. How did you dare enter such a royal house as this?
Polly We've come from another world. By magic.
Jadis (*to Digory*) Is this true?
Digory Yes, it is.
Jadis But you are no Magician. The mark of it is not on you. You can only be the Magician's servant. It is by another's magic you have travelled to this place.

Digory Yes, it was my Uncle Andrew. He's the Master Magician.

There is the rumble and crash of falling masonry

Jadis There is great peril here. The whole palace is breaking up. We must go before we are buried in the ruins. Come. (*She advances to the doors, raises her arm and makes to throw something at the doors*) Kabal kalumno.

The doors tremble as though made of silk and crumble to the floor. They reveal a great red dying sun low in a black sky. To the left of the sun and higher up is a single bright star

Has your uncle, the Master Magician, power such as mine? Well, I shall know that later. In the meantime, look both of you and learn. This is what happens to things and to people that stand in my way. What do you see?

Polly It's horrible. Horrible.

Digory Everything's dead and destroyed. A vast city ruined and empty, all the buildings crumbling to dust—even that huge river is dried up and full of dust.

Jadis What do you hear?

Digory Nothing. It's silent with death. There's nothing here alive.

Jadis There was once. This was Charn, the wonder of the world, the great city of the King of Kings. Once it was full of noise: the marching of armies; the shouts of commands; the thunder of chariots; the cracking of whips and the groaning of slaves; the sacrificial drums beating in the temples. Once, the roar of battle soared up from every street, and the great river of Charn ran red with blood. Then—all in one moment—one woman blotted it out for ever.

Digory Who?

Jadis Why, I. I, Jadis, the last Queen—the Queen of all the Worlds.

Polly How could you destroy a world in one moment?

Jadis By magic, child. Real magic. I knew the secret of the Deplorable Word.

Digory The what?

Jadis The Deplorable Word. The one word which if spoken with proper ceremonies will destroy all living things but the one who has spoken it.

Polly But how could you do that?

Jadis I had no other choice. The enemy army was about to win. The last of my soldiers had been killed. My accursed sister—

Digory You were fighting your sister?

Jadis Don't interrupt, child. My accursed sister and her rebels were about to take my throne, my city, my very world away from me. She stood there facing me, flashing her wicked eyes at me. "Victory." she said. "Yes", said I, "but not yours." And then I uttered the Deplorable Word. A moment later I was the only living thing beneath the sun. The victory was mine.

Digory But what about the people?

Jadis People? What people?

Polly The ordinary people. Not the soldiers but the women and children? And what about the animals?

Jadis (*to Digory*) Don't you understand? I am the Queen. They were all my people, my animals. To do with as I liked. But how could you be expected to understand that—you, a mere common child? The weight of the world is on our royal shoulders. Ours is a high and lonely destiny.

Digory So you destroyed your people. And then what?

Jadis I made a spell that allowed me to sleep with all my ancestors here, needing neither food nor fire, though it were for a thousand years—until one came and struck the bell, and wakened me to my destiny.

Digory Was it the Deplorable Word that made the sun die, too?

Jadis The sun has always been like that. For hundreds of thousands of years. Have you a different sun in your world?

Digory Yes, it's smaller and yellower and hotter.

Jadis A-a-aah. So yours is a younger world? Let us be going at once.

Digory ⎫
Polly ⎭ (*together*) Going where?

Jadis Where? Why, to your world, of course.

Polly You can't.

Jadis grabs Polly by the right hand

Jadis Can't?

Digory She means you can't mean—that is, we didn't know you wanted to go there.

Jadis Why else were you sent here—but to fetch me?

Digory I'm sure you wouldn't like our world at all. Our people wouldn't let your rule it, you know.

Jadis With my beauty and my Magic, I would have your world at my feet within a year. Do you doubt it?

Digory No, I don't, your Majesty. Polly, put your right hand into your pocket, Polly, and show Queen Jadis that picture you carry of our lovely green world.

Polly What?

Digory Think green, Polly! Put your right hand in your pocket so we can show the Queen what's what.

Jadis lets go of Polly's right hand

Digory Use the green ring, Polly. NOW!

There is a black-out, followed by a green light

Polly's Voice Digory! Are we safe?

Digory's Voice We're back in that strange green wood, again.

Polly's Voice The Wood Between The Worlds. But are we safe?

Digory's Voice I think so. Shall we stay here? I feel safe, anyway.

Polly's Voice Well, I don't. I feel wide—yes, wide awake.

Digory's Voice Why, Polly?

Polly's Voice Because you're holding on to my hair. Let go!

Digory's Voice I'm not touching you!

Polly's Voice It's her! It's Queen Jadis. She's grabbed my hair! Owwwww! Let go of me! What are you doing?

Digory's Voice Let go of her! Here, Polly, I'll help you. That's it! You're free! Go on! Change the rings. Now, quickly, get into the home pool. The one with the mark in the turf, remember? Keep good hold on my hand. That's right. Here we go. Just like swimming underwater. Ouch! I must have banged my ear. It really hurts. Oh no, oh no!

SCENE 4

The street outside Uncle Andrew's house, with the façades of several houses and a lamppost. The same wet summer evening

Polly, Digory and Jadis have arrived back in London. Jadis is holding on to Digory's ear

Digory Let go! Let go of my ear!
Jadis (*releasing him*) What place is this?
Polly This is where we live. That's my house and that's Digory's uncle's.
Jadis And where is the house of the Great Magician?
Digory It's here. This house, here.
Jadis This is not the house of a Great Magician, but that of a servant.

Uncle Andrew opens the front door and enters the street, approaching the three

Uncle Andrew Is that you children? Are you back? I thought I heard your voices—Good Lord! (*He sees Jadis and bows, rubbing his hands together*) W-W-W-Welcome M-M-M-M-M-M Madam. Good evening.
Jadis Is *this* the Magician who has called me into this world? It can't be.
Uncle Andrew (*still bowing*) Ah—ah—Madam. I am most honoured—highly gratified—a most unexpected pleasure—if only I had had the opportunity of making preparations—I would have ...
Jadis Where is the Magician, fool?
Uncle Andrew Madam, it is I. I am the Magician. I hope you will excuse any liberty these naughty children may have taken. I assure you there was no intention ...
Jadis You? You, the Magician? (*She grabs him by the hair and looks down at his face, studying it closely*) I see. You *are* a Magician—of a sort.

Jadis lets Uncle Andrew go, so suddenly that he falls down

Don't sprawl there. You are not speaking to your equal. I am Jadis, Queen of Queens, Ruler of Rulers, Queen of All The Worlds! How do *you* come to know magic? You are not of the royal blood, I'll swear.
Uncle Andrew Well, not strictly speaking, no. Not exactly royal. Although the Ketterleys are a very old family. From Dorsetshire, Ma'am.
Jadis Dorsetshire? Is that yet another world, Magician? No matter—I see what you really are. You are a little, peddling Magician who works by rules and systems and probably by books. There is no real magic in your blood and heart. Your kind was dealt with in my world a thousand years ago. Here, I shall allow you to be my servant.

Uncle Andrew I should be most happy—delighted to be of any service—a pleasure, I assure—

Jadis Silence, servant, you talk too much. Where exactly are we?

Uncle Andrew In London, Ma'am. The greatest city in the world.

Jadis Excellent. Procure for me a chariot or flying carpet or a well-trained dragon. Whatever is the usual transport for royal persons in your land.

Uncle Andrew I'll fetch my coat and some money and then I'll go and order a hansom cab at once.

Uncle Andrew makes to enter the house

Jadis Stop! Do not dream of treachery! My eyes will be on you wherever you go. At the first sign of disobedience you will be punished with fire and ice. Now go!

Uncle Andrew exits into the house

Jadis Once I have transport, then I will get the fool to take me to places where I can obtain jewels and suitable clothing. This world is even colder than mine. After that—

Polly (*to Digory*) We've got to stop her, Digory.

Uncle Andrew enters backwards from the house, pursued by Aunt Letitia

Uncle Andrew All I wanted, dear sister, was the temporary loan of five pounds.

Aunt Letitia I've told you times without number that I *will not* lend you money.

Uncle Andrew But you don't understand, Letty dear, it's most important. I have some quite unexpected expenses today. I have to do a little entertaining. Please don't be troublesome.

Aunt Letitia And whom, pray, are you going to entertain?

Uncle Andrew Why, a most distinguished visitor who has just arrived. Look here! (*He gestures towards Jadis*)

Jadis How long do I have to wait for my chariot, slave?

Aunt Letitia And who is this person, brother dear?

Uncle Andrew A distinguished foreigner. A very important person.

Aunt Letitia Dressed like that? Talking like that? Rubbish! Get away from my house this moment, you shameless hussy, or I'll send for the police.

Jadis Does this woman dare to threaten *me*? Down on your knees, minion, before I blast you.

Aunt Letitia I will not tolerate strong language. Get out of here!

Jadis flings out her arm at Aunt Letitia

Jadis Kabal kalumno!

Nothing happens

Aunt Letitia I thought so. She's drunk! She can't even speak clearly.

Jadis attacks Aunt Letitia, throwing her against the front door, stunning her. Then she turns to Uncle Andrew

Jadis Now slave, lead me to the chariot!
Uncle Andrew This violence is so needless—it's so regrettable . . .
Jadis Silence, slave!

Jadis and Uncle Andrew exit

Polly and Digory rush over to help Aunt Letitia, who is just coming round

Aunt Letitia Has she gone? Where is Andrew? Has he taken any money? What on earth has been going on? It's disgraceful! That woman's so strong—she must be drunk or mad. We must tell the police. Digory, see if you can find a constable. And who is *this* young person? Are you another of Andrew's disreputable companions?

Without answering, Digory moves defeatedly down the street in search of a constable

Polly I'm Polly from next door, Ma'am—a friend of Digory's.
Aunt Letitia Well, at least you have some manners.

A church bell strikes six

Six o'clock. Isn't it your dinner time? It certainly is for Digory, and for his poor, dear mother.
Polly How is Digory's mother? Is she very ill?
Aunt Letitia Very ill. I'm afraid food isn't much use, either. Nothing in *this* world will do her much good. She needs fruit from the land of youth to help her now.
Polly Fruit from the land of youth? I've never heard of that.
Aunt Letitia It's her only hope . . .

Digory returns

Ah! Digory.
Digory I can't see a constable anywhere, but I can hear the sound of galloping.

As he says this we too can hear the approach of galloping hooves

It's coming very fast. Is it a fire engine? It's getting very close!

The sound of galloping hooves grows louder, accompanied by the sound of whip lashes, panic-stricken neighing, and a shattering crash

Why , it's her!

Jadis enters with a frantic horse

Jadis Beast, you have dared to endanger Jadis, Queen of Queens. I will have you taken to the Bestial Chamber and torn apart by torturers.

Uncle Andrew enters, looking completely dishevelled and dazed, with his top hat rammed over his face

Uncle Andrew (*muffled*) What happened? What happened?

The sounds of more hooves, hubbub and pursuit

A Fat Man, a Cabby, Policeman 1, a man in a deerstalker hat (smoking a meerschaum, carrying a violin case and trying to get past without being noticed), an Errand Boy, Policeman 2, and a Soldier enter

Fat Man That's the woman! Do your duty, constable. Hundreds and thousands of pounds' worth she's taken from my shop.

Cabby Mr Pleeceman! Orficer! That's my 'orse what she's got 'old of. And it's my cab that she's made matchwood of. Stole it she did.

Fat Man What about my pearls and rings?

Policeman 1 One at a time, one at a time. Please—

Cabby But there ain't no time. I know that 'orse better than you. 'E ain't no ordinary 'orse. 'Is farver was a horficer's charger in the cavalry, 'e was. An' if the lady starts excitin' 'im anymore, there'll be murder done. 'Ere, let me get at 'im.

Policeman 1 Murder? Murder? Stolen jewels, stolen 'orses and now murder? This is all getting a bit beyond me. *(To the man in the deerstalker)* Perhaps you could give me a hand, sir?

The man in the deerstalker exits without replying

Oh, well . . .

Cabby *(approaching Jadis)* Now, Missy, let me get at 'is 'ead. Steady, Strawberry, old boy. Steady, now.

Jadis Dog! Dog, unhand our royal charger. We are the Empress Jadis.

Policeman 1 Silence, please. Now, Madam, per'aps you would care to tell me your side of this—

Jadis Tell you? I will do more than tell you! I will show you.

She rips the iron cross-bar from a nearby lamppost, and advances slowly on the policeman, pulling the horse, while the Cabby tries to ease the horse away from her

Policeman 1 Now, Madam, I'm warning you, assaulting a police officer is a most serious—

Errand Boy She's goin' ter bop 'im!

Polly Digory! We've got to stop her.

Digory We must do it together. I'll grab her. You do the ring. Remember, use the yellow one.

Jadis fells Policeman 1. Policeman 2 advances on her. She aims a blow at him. He retreats. The Soldier now advances. Policeman 2 joins him. Jadis is swinging the iron bar dangerously close to everyone, but still holding on to the Horse, which the Cabby is trying to calm

Errand Boy Let's chuck a few stones at 'er.

Jadis Scum! You shall pay dearly for this when I have conquered your world. Not one stone of your city will be left. I will make your weedy little village of Lundin as I made Felinda, as I made Sorlois, Bramandin and Charn! Nothing will be left!

Uncle Andrew My dear lady . . . you must not . . . *(he goes to Jadis and falls at her knees, holding her dress)*

Jadis Don't touch me, slave!

Polly Now, Digory, now! Grab her ankle!
Digory I've got her. Go, Polly, go.

A monstrous humming

Black-out

CURTAIN

ACT II

The Wood Between the Worlds

Uncle Andrew, Polly, Digory, Jadis, Cabby, and Strawberry, the horse, are all there

Uncle Andrew Where are we?

Polly Oh, no, Uncle Andrew, are you here?

Jadis Servant, are you there? I feel unwell.

Digory Polly! Thank goodness, I thought we'd lost touch.

Polly I'm fine. Queen Jadis and your Uncle Andrew are here. He's still hanging on to her dress.

Digory And Cabby and Strawberry are here. At least I think so. It looks like your Strawberry, but different somehow.

Cabby It's Strawberry, young sir. I'd know him anywhere. That's my boy, drink sweetly out of that pool. Why won't the lady let go of him?

Jadis Servant, get off your knees and fetch me water. I am unwell.

Uncle Andrew I'm feeling very faint myself. Is this delirium? It's not fair. I never wanted to be a Magician. Oh, my head.

Digory Polly, we've got to get Queen Jadis back to her own world while she's still holding onto us all. If she lets go, we've had it. We've got to change rings. Go to green.

Polly Green it is. Where are we going?

Digory Back to Charn, I hope. Now!

Humming noise

Green-out

Black-out

Narnia

Total darkness

Polly Are we there, yet?

Digory We seem to be somewhere. I'm standing on something solid.

Polly Why so am I, come to think of it. But why's it so dark? Do you think we got into the wrong pool?

Digory Perhaps this *is* Charn—only in the middle of the night.

Jadis This is not Charn, fool. This is an empty world. This is Nothing.

Uncle Andrew Polly! Digory! I've had enough of this nonsense. Get us out of here at once.

Cabby If I wuz you, sir, I wouldn't talk to them like that. They got us 'ere, so presoomably they're the ones who can get us back again. It would pay yer to be a bit more pleasant to them there kids.

Jadis In a World of Nothing, there is Nothing for me to control. I fear my Doom has come upon me. I feel most unwell.

Uncle Andrew Madam! Madam! Please, don't say things like that. It can't be as bad as all that. Cabman,—do you happen to have a flask of something about you? A drop of spirits, perhaps?

Polly Digory?

Digory Yes, Polly?

Polly Do you know what I think?

Digory No, Polly.

Polly I think the grown-ups have lost control. I think they're afraid of the dark.

Cabby Now then, now then. Keep cool everyone, that's what I say. Is everyone all right? No bones broken? Good. Well, that's something to be thankful for straight away, after falling all that way. Now where do we think we are? I expect we've fallen down some diggings in the road. Probably the new Underground station. Someone will be along shortly, I expect. Now, 'ow are we going to pass the time while we wait for 'elp? I know, let's sing a 'ymn. A good 'ymn always cheers yer up. 'Ere we go.

> "Come, ye thankful people, come,
> Raise the song of harvest home.
> All be safely gathered in,
> Ere the winter storms begin."

Come on everyone, join in!

Polly
Digory } (*together*)

> "God, our Maker, doth provide
> For our wants to be supplied;
> Come to God's own temple, come;
> Raise the song of harvest home."

Cabby Now that was cheerin', wasn't it? Shall we do another?

Uncle Andrew (*sotto voce, to Digory*) Digory! Now, my boy. Slip on your ring. Let's be off.

Jadis Fool! Have you forgotten I can hear even men's thoughts? Let the boy go! If you attempt treachery, I will take such vengeance on you as never was heard of in all the worlds from the beginning.

Digory And, Uncle Andrew, if you think I'd be so mean as to leave Polly and the Cabby, and Strawberry in a place like this—you're very badly mistaken.

Uncle Andrew And you, Digory, are a naughty and impertinent little boy!

Polly Hush! Listen!

A deep voice can be heard singing from far away

Digory Is that you singing, Cabby? You sound a long way away.
Cabby No, young feller, it's not me.
Polly Where's it coming from?
Digory There!
Cabby No, there!
Polly It's everywhere!
Cabby Gawd! Ain't it lovely?

Other voices join in, in harmony: cold, tinkling, silvery voices. Stars suddenly blaze in the sky

Digory Look, the Deep Voice has made the stars come out.
Polly And the stars are singing, too.
Cabby Glory be! I'd 'ave been a better man all my life, if I'd aknown there were things like this.

The Deep Voice is louder, the star song fading

Polly What's happening now?
Digory The sky's turning grey. Can you feel the wind on your cheeks? Are those hills over there?
Polly I can see your face now. Why's Uncle Andrew so frightened? And look at the Queen—she hates it!
Cabby Now the sky's white, pink, gold.
Polly The Deep Voice is getting louder and louder!
Digory Oh, look, just look! *Sunrise!*

A young bright sun has risen. It lights up Narnia—a valley through which a broad river flows towards the sun. To the north hills, to the south mountains. But it's a valley of rock, earth and water

Cabby And there's the Deep Voice.

   Aslan, the Lion, enters

Polly It's a Lion!
Uncle Andrew Get him away! Get him away from me! DO SOMETHING!!
Jadis Take this, Lion!

Jadis throws the iron bar at Aslan. It hits him without any visible effect and falls to the ground

Cabby She 'it 'im.
Digory He didn't even flinch. But I bet he's really angry now.

   Jadis screams with anger, frustration and fear and exits

Uncle Andrew turns to run and falls flat on his face

   The Lion brushes past the children and Cabby, ignores them, and, still singing, exits

Polly Oh, how sad. I wish he'd stayed.

Uncle Andrew Now, Digory. We've got to get rid of that woman and that brute of a lion has gone, too. Give me your hand and put on your ring at once.

Digory Keep away! Keep clear of him, Polly. Come over here, beside me. I warn you Uncle Andrew, don't come one step nearer.

Uncle Andrew Do what you're told this minute, sir.

Digory I won't. Polly and I want to stay here and see what happens.

Uncle Andrew You're an extremely disobedient, ill-behaved little boy.

Digory Uncle Andrew, don't you want to know about other worlds? Don't you like it now you're here?

Uncle Andrew Like it? Like it? Just look at the state I'm in! And this was my best coat—and my best waistcoat, too. I'm not saying that it's not interesting being here. Something might be made of this country. The air is delightful—fresh and sort of, well, young. It might even have done my failing health some good. Apart from that Lion, of course—dangerous-looking beast. If only we had a gun.

Cabby Gun be blowed. I think I'll go and give Strawberry a rub-down and a chat. 'E's got more sense than some humans as I could mention.

Cabby and Strawberry exit

Digory Do you really think the Lion could be killed by a gun? He didn't mind the iron bar much when Jadis threw it at him.

Uncle Andrew She's a spirited gel, that Queen Jadis. It was a plucky thing to do.

Polly It was a wicked thing to do. What harm had the Lion done to her?

Digory Here, Polly, look at this!

Polly What is it? Oh, look, it's a perfectly made tiny little lamppost.

As they look on, the mini-lamppost grows larger

Digory And it's growing bigger all the time.

Polly And it's alive. I mean, it's all lit up, too.

Uncle Andrew Remarkable! Remarkable! I never dreamt of magic like this. We've discovered a world where everything is bursting with life and growth. The commercial possibilities are unbounded. If this lamppost can grow from just a bit of another lamppost, then I could bring a few bits of old scrap-iron here, bury them in the ground, and they'd come up as brand new railway engines, or battleships, girder-bridges, perhaps even those new-fangled horseless carriages. They'd actually cost me nothing to make, but I could use the rings to take them all and sell them at their full market value back in England. I'd be a millionaire in no time.

Digory What are you talking about, Uncle?

Uncle Andrew And if this beautiful place makes *me* feel years younger, why shouldn't it work for other people? Think of all the people this place would help. Just think of it: you could bring them on a trip to the land of youth.

Digory Oh! The land of youth! Do you really think it is? Do you think there's anything here that would cure mother?

Uncle Andrew Digory, this isn't a chemist's shop, you silly little boy. As I was saying . . .

Digory You don't care tuppence about my mother, do you? And she's your sister, too. Well, I don't care about you, either. I'm going to find that Lion and ask if he can help me.

Polly Me, too.

Aslan enters

Uncle Andrew (*not seeing Aslan*) You're mad, the pair of you. How could a Lion possibly help you? You'd be better off . . . (*He notices Aslan*) Oh!

Digory Excuse me, Lion, I wonder whether you . . .

Aslan stares at him, and then turns away and begins to sing. The song is wilder, more passionate than before

Polly What's happening? What's he doing now?

Digory What a wonderful sound. It makes me want to jump and run and shout.

Polly And climb and rush at people and hug them.

Digory Or fight them.

Polly You've gone all red in the face.

Digory So has Uncle Andrew.

Uncle Andrew That Jadis is a demned fine gel. High spirited. It's a pity about her bad temper. But she's a dem fine figure of a woman.

Digory Look at the grass. It's . . . well, it's bubbling.

Polly Like boiling water in a saucepan.

Uncle Andrew I don't like the look of this.

Digory That bubble looks like a mole-hill. No, it's growing bigger and bigger.

Uncle Andrew And still growing. It's going to burst. I think we'd better go. Now.

Polly Don't be a coward. Stand still and watch. Something wonderful is happening.

Digory It's turned into a most beautiful reindeer.

Unnoticed by the others, a Rabbit, Jackdaw, Bulldog, Owl and Beaver enter and walk towards Aslan

Polly And there's another. And look at those two little bubbles. Pop! Pop! Two frogs!

Uncle Andrew And over there: panthers, leopards and giraffes.

Digory Cats, dogs, mice, sheep, cows . . . All the animals in the world.

Polly What's falling out of the trees? Oh, they're birds—all different kinds of birds.

Digory And butterflies.

Uncle Andrew That bubble's as big as a house. Here it goes. Bang! That's incredible—it's an elephant.

The song of the Lion is submerged beneath the sound of cawing, cooing, crowing, braying, neighing, baying, barking, lowing, bleating and trumpeting. The noise reaches a crescendo and stops. Silence

Cabby (*off*) 'Ere. Come back 'ere.

A different, revitalised Strawberry enters, followed by the Cabby

Cabby Strawberry! What's got into yer? Whoa there! Whoa up!

Strawberry ignores him and joins the other animals, who are forming into a circle around Aslan

Cabby 'E's 'opeless. This air's got ter 'im or sumfing.
Digory And he looks really different. Younger and better.

There is the cold, silvery tinkling sound of the stars

Aslan Narnia. Narnia. Narnia. Awake. Love. Think. Speak. Be talking beasts. Be walking trees. Be divine waters.
Animals (*together*) Hail, Aslan. Hail, great Lion.
Rabbit We hear.
Jackdaw We obey.
Strawberry We are awake.
Bulldog We love.
Owl We think.
Beaver We speak.
All Together We know.
Strawberry But please, Aslan, we don't know very much yet.
Aslan Creatures, I give you yourselves. I, Aslan, give to you forever this land of Narnia. I give you the woods, the fruits, the rivers. You will find fauns, satyrs, dwarves and giants in this land. Watch and learn from them. I give you the stars and I give you the dumb beasts—the animals that cannot talk. Treat them gently and cherish them. But do not go back to their ways lest you lose the power of speech. Remember, that out of them you were chosen and into them you can return. Do not do so.

There is silence for a few beats, then

Jackdaw No fear, sir! (*He realises he has spoken into silence*) Ooops! Oh, how embarrassing!

Animals start to laugh, hesitantly

Aslan Laugh and fear not, creatures. Now that you are no longer dumb, you need not always be grave. Jokes as well as justice come with the power of speech.

The animals laugh more freely

Jackdaw Aslan! Aslan! Have I made the first joke? Will everybody always be told how I made the first joke?
Aslan No, little friend Jackdaw, you have not *made* the first joke. You have *been* the first joke!

Animals laugh

And now Narnia is established. We must next take thought for keeping it safe. I wish to create my Council. The Chief Dwarf, the God of the Rivers, and the Major Oak will form part of it. Of the talking animals, I want the Owl, both the Ravens, and the Bull Elephant. The Council must meet straightaway. For although this world is only five hours' old, an Evil has already entered it. Come, Owl, we must talk together.

Aslan and the Owl exit

Digory I've got to follow him. If he can do all this, then he can surely help my sick mother. (*He moves towards Strawberry and the other animals Aslan has left behind*)

Uncle Andrew Digory, I forbid you! Those animals will slaughter every one of us.

Cabby Well, *I* don't reckon as 'ow they will. (*To Polly and Digory*) Come on, you two.

Polly, Digory, and Cabby walk towards the animals

Beaver What, in the name of Aslan, are you three things? Perhaps you're Neevils?

Cabby Well, we're, er . . .

Rabbit They look like a large kind of very tasty lettuce—

Uncle Andrew I told you! I warned you!

Polly No, we're not lettuce. In fact we're not at all nice to eat. Any of us.

Bulldog And, by the way, whoever heard of a talking lettuce? Oh, well. Bad luck, Rabbit.

Jackdaw Perhaps they're the second joke?

Rabbit Well, if they are, they're not as good as the first one. I don't see anything funny about them at all. I think we ought to eat them anyway.

Digory Please let us pass. I have to talk with the Lion.

Cabby And I want a word with that old 'orse of mine. (*He goes up to Strawberry*) Strawberry, old friend! You know me. You ain't going to stand there and say as you don't know me?

Beaver What's the Thing talking about, Horse?

Strawberry Well, I don't exactly know. Like most of us, I don't know a great deal about anything, yet. But I have seen a sort of Thing like this before. I think.

Cabby What? Yer don't know me? Me that fed yer of an evenin'; looked arter yer when it was cold; gave yer good fresh 'ay to lie in every day? Yer don't know me?

Strawberry Well, I remember you used to tie a horrid black thing to me, and then hit me to make me run, and then this black thing would rattle rattle after me. And I could never get away from it. And you were always sitting up on top of the black thing—while I did all the work.

Cabby A 'ard crool world. Pavin' stones an' cobble-stones. Far too 'ard for an 'orse—that's London, orl right. An' far too 'ard for me, too. You were a country 'orse, an' I was a country bloke. But there wasn't a living in the country.

Digory Please, please—the Lion's miles away by now. We must get on.

Jackdaw You won't catch Aslan, now.

Rabbit Not that he'd want to talk with two-leggers like you, anyway.

Polly But he's got to, you see.

Bulldog Why has he got to?

Cabby Well this lad 'ere 'as somethin' on his mind abaht his poor sick muvver as 'e wants to talk over wiv' Aslan.

Rabbit A sick mother, eh? Well, that might be different. What do you think, Beaver?

Beaver If it's about a sick mother, then we should let them pass.

Jackdaw Though Aslan will be leagues away by now.

Cabby (*to Strawberry*) Suppose you wuz to allow this young genn'lman to ride on your back, Strawberry? And trot 'im along to where the Lion is? This young lidy an' me can foller on be'ind.

Strawberry If it's about a sick mother ... well, of course. Come on, young feller-me-lad. Hop up. We'll be off straight away. Can you see which way the Lion and the Council went?

Digory (*pointing*) That must be them.

Strawberry, Digory, Polly and Cabby exit

Jackdaw (*looking over at Uncle Andrew*) And there's another of those two-leggers standing by itself over there.

Rabbit Well, he can't be one of the Horse's friends, or he wouldn't be on his own.

Beaver Perhaps he's the Neevil.

Bulldog We'd better go and find out.

They walk towards Uncle Andrew

Hello two-legger, are those your friends?

Uncle Andrew Oh, no. Look at that huge dog—growling and snarling at me.

Beaver Because if they are, you'd better catch them up.

Uncle Andrew And that nasty Beaver gnashing his teeth at me. Oh no. What can I do?

Jackdaw You'd better get a move on.

Uncle Andrew I hate birds. Nasty fluttering things. Go away! GO AWAY! You're nasty and dirty and vile and evil!

Beaver What's he saying?

Bulldog I think he said that he's over thirty and he's the Neevil.

Rabbit Right lads, we'd better get him!

A chase, which ends in the capture of Uncle Andrew, who promptly faints

Beaver The two-legger's fallen over.

Jackdaw It can't be a Neevil. It must be a walking tree.

Bulldog (*sniffing*) It smells like an animal.

Jackdaw An animal wouldn't just roll over like that.

Rabbit Animals don't roll over. They stand upright. Like me. (*He takes a step backward and falls over*)

Bulldog Oh, shut up, you stupid rabbit!

Jackdaw A joke! The third joke!

Beaver I think Jackdaw's right—it's definitely a tree.

Rabbit Well, if it's a tree, it shouldn't be left out here with its roots all exposed. It ought to be planted.

Jackdaw Where?

Beaver Over there looks like a good place. If you dig the hole, Bulldog, I'll get the water. Rabbit, Jackdaw, you two can get some straw and stuff for the roots. Now, all together, lift up the tree and off we go.

Bulldog, Beaver, Rabbit, and Jackdaw exit, carrying Uncle Andrew

SCENE 3

Another part of Narnia

Aslan and the Owl are in conference

Strawberry and Digory enter

Aslan I think that is about as far as we can plan, Owl. I will take up your suggestion about sending out patrols of birds to find the Witch ... (*He sees Digory*) Ah, I have been expecting you.

Digory Please, Mr Lion—Aslan—sir, could I have some magic fruit from this country to make my mother well again?

Aslan You'll be interested to know, Owl, that this is the boy. The boy who did it.

Digory Oh dear, what have I done now?

Aslan Son of Adam, there is an evil Witch abroad in my new land of Narnia. Tell us how she came here.

Digory I brought her here, Aslan.

Aslan For what purpose?

Digory I wanted to get her wickedness out of my world and back to her own. I thought I was taking her back.

Aslan How did she come to be in your world, Son of Adam?

Digory By magic.

Aslan Tell me what happened, my son.

Digory My uncle sent us—that's Polly and me—out of our own world by magic rings, and then we met the Witch in a place called Charn ...

Aslan You met the Witch?

Digory Well, actually, I woke her up. Accidentally. Well, I wanted to know what would happen if I struck a bell. Polly didn't want me to, and tried to stop me, but I fought her ... I must have been enchanted.

Aslan Must you?

Digory Well, no. I'm just pretending. (*Pause*) I see. I've spoiled everything. There's no chance of getting help for Mother now.

Aslan You see, Owl, that before the new clean world I gave you is more than seven hours old, a force of evil has entered it. A force awakened and brought here by this Son of Adam. (*To Digory*) But do not be cast down. Evil will come of the evil, but it is still a long way off. I will see to it that the worst falls on myself. So now, let us make this a merry land in a merry world for many hundreds of years. And as Adam's race has done the harm, so Adam's race shall help to mend it.

Cabby and Polly enter

(*Addressing Cabby and Polly*) Draw near, you two. (*To the Cabby*) My son, I have known you long. Do you know me?

Cabby Well, no, sir. Leastways, not in an ordinary manner of speaking. Yet I feel as 'ow we 'ave met before.

Aslan It is well. You know better than you think you know, and you shall live to know me better yet. How does this land please you?

Cabby It's a fair treat, sir.

Aslan Would you like to live here always?

Cabby Well, sir, I would sir, but for one fing. I'm a newly married man, sir. If my wife was here, I reckon neither of us would ever want to go back to London again, and that's the truth.

Aslan roars a summons. Nellie, the Cabby's wife, appears, dressed in an apron, with her sleeves rolled up, her arms covered in soapsuds. She sees Aslan and curtseys, then goes to the Cabby and holds his hand

Nellie Cor, where am I?

Cabby improvizes an answer for Nellie

Aslan My son. You and your wife are to be the first King and Queen of Narnia. You shall rule all the creatures, and do justice among them, and protect them from their enemies, when enemies arise. And enemies will arise, for there is an evil Witch already in this world.

Cabby Begging your pardon, sir, and thanking you very much I'm sure—yes indeed, sir, thank you very much—but I ain't no sort of chap for a job like that. I never 'ad much eddycation.

Aslan Can you use a spade and a plough and raise food from the earth?

Cabby Yes sir. That I can. I'm country born and bred.

Aslan Can you rule the creatures kindly and fairly?

Cabby I'd try to do the square thing by them all, as I've allus done, sir.

Aslan And would you bring up your children and grandchildren to do the same?

Cabby We'd certainly do our best: wouldn't we, Nellie?

Nellie nods agreement

Aslan And if enemies came, would you be first in the charge and last in the retreat?

Cabby Well sir, to be truthful, I never did no fightin' except with me fists. But I'd try to do me bit.

Aslan Then you will have done all that a King should do. You and your wife will be crowned King and Queen, later. (*To Polly*) Now, Daughter of Eve, you are welcome to my Narnia. Have you forgiven the boy for fighting with you in the Hall of Queens at Charn?

Polly Of course I have, Aslan.

Aslan That is well. That is very well. So, now for the boy himself. (*To Digory*) Son of Adam, are you ready to undo the wrong you have done to my sweet country of Narnia?

Digory Well, yes. Of course. But I don't know—

Aslan I asked: are you ready?

Digory Yes, yes. But please will you give me something that can help my mother? She is so ill, and it's all so sad and—

Aslan My son, grief is hard to bear. Only you and I know that yet. You think of your mother. But I have to think of hundreds of creatures and hundreds of years in the life of Narnia. It is my wish to plant a tree here that the Witch will not dare approach. A tree that will protect Narnia from her for many, many years. You must get me the seed from which that tree is to grow.

Digory Yes, sir. I don't know how, but I will.

Aslan I will tell you how. Turn to the West, and tell me what you see.

Digory I see huge mountains and a river coming down vast cliffs in a steaming waterfall.

Aslan The land of Narnia ends at that waterfall. You must make your way there. Once at the top of the cliffs, you will be out of Narnia and into the Western Wild. You must journey through the mountains until you find a green valley with a blue lake in it walled around by ice. At the end of the lake is a steep green hill. On the top of that hill is a garden. In the centre of the garden is a tree. Pluck an apple from that tree and bring it back to me.

Digory Yes, sir. It will take me considerable time.

Aslan You shall have help. Horse, would you like wings?

Strawberry What me? A winged horse? Why, yes—but I'm not a very clever horse.

Aslan You shall be the father of all flying horses. You will have a new name. You are to be known as Fledge.

Strawberry Fledge, eh? That's a proud name—ooh, my back is itching. Just behind my shoulder blades. Ow, it's really painful.

Cabby It's all right, Strawb—I mean Fledge; I'll rub the pain away.

Fledge Thank you, thank you. It's like swollen fetters on my back—Ow!

Polly Don't worry, Fledge. We're here. Oh, look!

Digory He's growing wings!

Aslan Is it good, Fledge?

Fledge It is good, Aslan.

Aslan Now carry the boy to the mountain valley.

Nellie and Polly are conferring off to one side

(*To Nellie and Polly*) What is the matter, Daughters of Eve?

Nellie Begging your pardon, sir, but I think the little girl would love to go, too.

Aslan What do you say, Fledge?

Fledge I can carry two—as long as they're little ones.

Aslan Then begone, with my blessing.

Fledge, Digory and Polly exit

Aslan Do not fly too high. Fly between the mountains, not over them. There will always be a way through. Now, Owl, let us go with our new King and Queen and discuss their coronation. First we must decide upon their names . . .

Aslan, Cabby, Nellie and Owl exit

Black-out

SCENE 4

The skies above Narnia

Fledge, Digory and Polly enter

Digory Oh, Fledge. This is fun. Hold on to me tight, Polly.
Polly Look down there! See the rocks and heath and the tiny trees? There's the river, like silver ribbon.
Digory Look ahead! Look at those great cliffs. And that huge waterfall.

The crashing sound of the waterfall can be heard as they pass over it

Polly Listen to it. Listen to the thunder.
Digory It's very strange—but I can smell something really delicious. Coming up from the ground.
Polly Where?
Digory There. Among those trees on that little hill. Look, there's a blue lake!
Polly And the icy mountains all around. Just like Aslan said. That must be the place!
Fledge Thank goodness.
Polly (*pointing*) What's that?
Digory What?
Polly I thought I saw someone move.
Digory Did you see anything, Fledge?
Fledge Nothing at all. Get ready to land, now. Hold on really tight.
Polly I must have been mistaken.

Black-out

SCENE 5

The Orchard of the Silver Apple Tree

Digory enters

Digory This has to be the place. I wish Polly and Fledge were here, it's a bit lonely without them. But they did say it was best to go alone. There's some writing on that notice there. What does it say? "Trespassers will be prosecuted" or "Keep off the grass", I bet. No, it's a poem.

"Come in by the golden gates or not at all.

Take of my fruit for others or forbear.
For those who steal or those who climb my wall
Shall find their heart's desire and then despair."

Well, *I'm* all right. I came in by the golden gates and I'm taking the fruit
for Aslan, not for me. Now let's take an apple. Just one apple, like Aslan
said, and then I'll be off. (*He picks an apple from the tree and pockets it*)

Jadis enters from behind the tree, eating an apple

Digory You! How did you get here?
Jadis Over the wall that surrounds this orchard, slave.
Digory Not by the gates?
Jadis What gates?
Digory And you've eaten an apple!
Jadis I was hungry, boy. And when I'm hungry I take what I need.
Digory You didn't read the notice?
Jadis Read? Read a notice? Me? Why should I read a notice? I am a Queen.
I make notices.

Digory turns to go

No, don't try to run away from me. I mean you no harm. If you do not
stop and listen to me now, you will miss some knowledge that would have
made you happy all your life.
Digory I don't think I want to hear this.
Jadis I know what errand you have come on, now. You are taking that
apple back to the Lion, for him to eat, for him to use. You are a fool! A
simpleton! Do you know what that fruit is? I will tell you. It is the apple of
youth, the apple of life.
Digory And you dared to eat one?
Jadis Of course I dared to eat it. I know now that I shall never grow old or
die. Why don't you eat yours, and then we will both live forever and be
the immortal King and Queen of this world, or your world, or whichever
world we choose.
Digory No, thank you. I wouldn't want to live after everyone I know is
dead. I'd rather live an ordinary time and go to Heaven.
Jadis Then what about this mother of yours?
Digory What's she got to do with it?
Jadis Just one bite of that apple would make her well again. Use your magic
rings. Go back to your own world. Give your mother the fruit. Soon, she
will be well again. You will be happy—like other boys.
Digory Oh, I'd love to make my mother well again. But I have to help the
Lion, haven't I?
Jadis Why? What has he done for you? What can he do to you once you are
safe at home? And what would your mother think if she found out that
you could have made her well and whole again, but that you preferred to
run errands for a wild animal in a strange world that is no business of
yours?
Digory But I made a promise.

Jadis A promise made in ignorance is no real promise. And who is here' to stop you?

Digory My mother's very strict about promises. She'd stop me if she were here.

Jadis But she's not. And she need never know. No one in your whole world need know anything. You don't even need to take that little girl back with you.

Digory What, leave Polly behind? My friend, Polly? What are you saying? Why are you so precious fond of my mother all of a sudden? What's it got to do with you? What's your game?

Jadis No game, child. Games have rules.

Digory And you want me to break all the rules, don't you?

Jadis Go back to your Lion, fool. Go back with your silly little friend to your sick mother and watch her die. When you are old and weak and dying, remember how you threw away the chance of endless youth. It won't be offered you again. And you can tell your precious Lion that I, Jadis, Queen of All the Worlds, am now one of the immortals. Tell him I am all-powerful.

Digory (*shouting*) You'll never beat Aslan! Not in a thousand years!

Jadis You tell Aslan I will use my power to take his new country from him and turn it into a wasteland.

Jadis exits

Polly and Fledge enter

Polly We heard everything. You are so brave. Digory. If only Aslan could have been here to see . . .

Aslan, Cabby (King Frank), Nellie (Queen Helen)—these last two robed but not yet crowned, and their entourage, including Rabbit, Bulldog, Jackdaw, Beaver and a Mess (a.k.a. Uncle Andrew) enter

Aslan But I am here, Polly. We are all here. Now, Digory?

Digory I have found the apple you wanted, sir.

Aslan Well done. You have found the protection of Narnia. Now we can proceed to crown our King and Queen.

Rabbit Sir! Sir!

Aslan Yes?

Rabbit, Bulldog, Jackdaw and Beaver step forward with a Mess

Rabbit Well, sir, we found this thing and decided it was a tree and needed planting.

Bulldog I still think it smells like an animal.

Jackdaw Oh shut up! You're so . . . so dogmatic!

Rabbit We all decided it was a Neevil tree and planted it. Then Beaver watered it and it seemed to wake up and scream and howl and wave its branches around a bit.

Beaver So we decided it must be a walking tree, and dug it up again, and sure enough it tried to run away. That made us pretty sure it was a Neevil.

Bulldog So we caught it, and put a net around it.

Rabbit To keep it safe until you, sir, could see it and decide what it was properly and then decide what to do with it.

Aslan Bring out the creature.

Uncle Andrew is brought forward, shivering with fear

Polly (*to Aslan*) Can you say something to unfrighten him? And then say something to stop him ever coming here again?

Aslan Do you think he wants to?

Polly He might send someone else like he sent us. He got so excited about the lamppost growing from the iron cross-bar and he thinks . . .

Aslan He thinks foolishness, child. This world bursts with life because my song still hangs in the air. It will not be so for long. And I cannot tell him anything: all he can hear are growls and roars. But I will give him one gift. (*He breathes on Uncle Andrew*) Sleep. Sleep and be safe from all the torments you have devised for yourself.

Uncle Andrew falls asleep

Aslan Take him aside, creatures. Now, where are the crowns?

Two Animals enter bringing forward two simple crowns on cushions. One is set with rubies, the other with emeralds

(*To Cabby and Nellie*) Step forward. Kneel before me. Tell us by what names you wish to be known.

Cabby My wife will be known as Queen Helen.

Nellie My husband will be known as King Frank.

Aslan places the crowns on their heads

Aslan Rise up, King and Queen of Narnia, father and mother of many kings that shall be. Be just and merciful and brave. The blessing is upon you.

All Hail the Queen! Hail the King!

Aslan And now, Digory, give the apple to the King for him to plant and make grow into a tree. For the tree will be the shield that makes Narnia safe from the Witch. Take the apple, King of Narnia, take your Queen and your people, and live in happiness. Narnia for ever!

King, Queen, and some members of their entourage exit to shouts of:

All Narnia for ever! Long live the Queen! Long live the King!

Aslan Digory! You seem down at heart.

Digory I forgot to tell you something, Aslan. The Witch ate one of those apples.

Aslan How did she do that?

Digory She climbed over the wall and took one to eat, because she was hungry.

Aslan So she ignored the notice.

Digory Yes.

Aslan And that is why the tree will always be a shield. She broke the rules and ate the apple—at the wrong time and in the wrong way. She will hate the taste and smell of those apples for the rest of her life.

Polly But she'll live for ever.

Aslan And she'll be miserable for ever. Living for ever with an evil heart means living in misery. And already she begins to know it.

Digory I nearly ate one myself, I was so hungry.

Aslan And you nearly took an apple for another reason, did you not?

Digory Yes, Aslan, the Witch wanted me to take an apple home for my mother.

Aslan And if you had it would have made your mother well again, but in such a way that you would have both looked back and wished she could have died in that illness.

Digory So there is no hope. My mother has to die.

Aslan There is always hope. That is what would have happened with a stolen apple. Now, go! Pluck an apple from the tree. It will not give endless life in your world, but it will make the ill well again. Take one with my blessing.

Polly And what now, Aslan? Please, may we go home now?

Aslan Of course, child. Of course. And bring your Uncle over here beside me. Stand together and hold his hands.

Polly and Digory do so

Black-out

Digory's Voice What about the rings?

Polly's Voice I can't find mine. I must have dropped them.

Aslan's Voice You need no rings when I am with you. I have two more things to say. A warning and a command. Let your world beware. It may be that some wicked person in your world will find a secret as devastating as the Deplorable Word. Watch out at all times and do not let your world be ruled by tyrants who care no more for justice and mercy than does the Empress Jadis. That is the warning. The command is that you take the magic rings away from your Uncle and bury them so that no-one will find them ever again.

Digory's Voice Will we see you again, Aslan?

Aslan's Voice Perhaps ... perhaps ...

Scene 6

Mother's Room in London

Mother is in bed asleep

Digory enters, followed by Polly

Digory Sssshh! She's asleep.

Polly Is she any better?

Digory I don't know. I cut the apple into pieces and gave it all to her as soon as I got back.

Polly What? All of it? All the core, too?

Digory No, I buried the core out in the garden.

Polly I thought she couldn't eat anything.

Digory Yes, that was strange. When I came into the room with the apple it began to sort of glow and then ... Do you remember when we were flying with Fledge and that wonderful smell coming up from the orchard? Well, this room smelled like that, only ten times better. Then Mother woke up and said something.

Polly What did she say?

Digory I didn't hear. But I fed her the bits of the apple. And she took them very easily. Then she turned over and fell asleep. Without any medicine. For the first time. And she's been asleep ever since.

Polly She looks very peaceful. By the way, what did you do with your rings?

Digory I buried them along with all the ones that were left.

Polly Where?

Digory I'm not telling you. What did you do with yours?

Polly I threw them on the fire. It was like indoor fireworks. How's Uncle Andrew?

Digory When he woke up after he got back, he locked himself in his room.

Polly Is he making more magic?

Digory I don't think so. He sent all his books out to be sold.

Aunt Letitia enters

Aunt Letitia And a very good thing, too. Now, what are you two doing here?

Digory I brought Polly in to see how Mother was. Aunt Letitia, what did the doctor say?

Aunt Letitia He said it was most extraordinary. That it was like a miracle. But he didn't want to raise any false hopes. We won't know anything until she wakes up.

Digory And when will that be?

Aunt Letitia Well, maybe soon.

Digory Or maybe ... not. Maybe never ...

Aunt Letitia We've had some good news, anyway. Your father is on his way home.

Digory Father? On his way home! Oh, thank goodness!

Polly It's going to be all right.

Digory I know Father's coming home, but that doesn't make Mother better.

Polly It's going to be all right. Listen!

The sound of a large cat purring

Can you hear? It's Aslan.

Digory Aslan, here?

Aunt Letitia It's a cat. I can hear a cat purring. A cat's got into the bedroom. We must find it and shoo it out.

Digory I don't think it's the kind of cat you can shoo out, Aunt Letitia. It's a bit too big for that!

Aunt Letitia Are you playing silly games, Digory? Polly, have you brought a cat into the room?

Polly Well, you see . . . Oh, look!

Mother is stirring

Mother Digory! Is that you?

Digory Mother!

Mother (*sits up carefully*) And you Letitia?

Aunt Letitia Oh, my dear!

Mother And who is this little girl?

Polly I'm Polly from next door.

Aunt Letitia How are you feeling, my dear?

Mother Do you know, I am feeling very well. I'm feeling very well, indeed.

As the others move towards her, the purring stops and we hear the roar of the Lion

CURTAIN

FURNITURE AND PROPERTY LIST

Only essential items are listed below. Further items can be added at the director's discretion.

ACT I

SCENE 1

On stage: High-backed chair
Table. *On it:* green and yellow rings; gloves

SCENE 2

On stage: Nil

Personal: **Polly:** yellow ring (required throughout)
Digory: green and yellow rings (required throughout)

SCENE 3

On stage: Elaborately-dressed figures (including at least one live one, Jadis)
Pillar topped with an arch and bell
Hammer
Two large doors

SCENE 4

On stage: Lamppost
House facade—front door

Off stage: Meerschaum, violin case **(Man in deerstalker hat)**

ACT II

SCENE 1

On stage: Nil

Personal: **Jadis:** iron cross-bar from lamppost (I, iv)

SCENE 2

On stage: Nil

Personal: **Jadis:** iron cross-bar

SCENE 3

On stage: Nil

SCENE 4

On stage: Nil

SCENE 5

On stage: Apple tree (with at least one apple on it)
Posted notice or sign

Off stage: Apple **(Jadis)**
Two crowns, one set with rubies and the other with emeralds
(brought in by two animals, residents of Narnia)

SCENE 6

On stage: Bed

LIGHTING PLOT

Practical fittings required: nil

Various simple interior and exterior settings on an open stage

ACT I

To open: Warm interior light—evening

Cue 1	**Uncle Andrew:** "... the sooner you'll be back." *Green light*	(Page 5)
Cue 2	To open SCENE 2 *Bring up lighting*	(Page 5)
Cue 3	**Digory:** "One—two—three, jump." *Darkness, then whirling lights, a red glow, and then the light settles down*	(Page 7)
Cue 4	To open SCENE 3 *Bring up reddish light from a setting sun against an otherwise black sky*	(Page 7)
Cue 5	The doors ... crumble to the floor. *Intensify red, dying sunlight; bring up light as from a single bright star*	(Page 9)
Cue 6	**Digory:** "... green ring, Polly NOW!" *Black-out. Green light*	(Page 10)
Cue 7	To open SCENE 4 *Bring up warm exterior evening light*	(Page 11)
Cue 8	A monstrous humming *Black-out*	(Page 15)

ACT II

Cue 9	To open SCENE 1 *Bring up exterior lighting*	(Page 16)
Cue 10	Humming noise *Green-out, then after a few seconds: Black-out*	(Page 16)
Cue 11	To open SCENE 2 *Total darkness, brightening when scene established*	(Page 16)
Cue 12	Cold, tinkling, silvery voices *Bring up bright star-shine*	(Page 18)
Cue 13	**Digory:** "The sky's turning grey." *Cross fade to greyish lighting*	(Page 18)

| *Cue* 14 | **Cabby:** "Now the sky's white, pink, gold." | (Page 18) |
| | *Cross fade to white, then pink, then gold lighting* | |

| *Cue* 15 | **Digory:** "Oh, look, just look! Sunrise! | (Page 18) |
| | *Bring up bright sunlight* | |

| *Cue* 16 | To open SCENE 3 | (Page 24) |
| | *Bring up bright sunlight* | |

| *Cue* 17 | Aslan, Cabby, Nellie and Owl exit | (Page 27) |
| | *Black-out* | |

| *Cue* 18 | To open SCENE 4 | (Page 27) |
| | *Bring up bright sunlight* | |

| *Cue* 19 | **Polly:** "I must have been mistaken." | (Page 27) |
| | *Black-out* | |

| *Cue* 20 | To open SCENE 5 | (Page 27) |
| | *Bring up bright sunlight* | |

| *Cue* 21 | **Aslan:** "... hold his hands." (*Polly and Digory do so*) | (Page 31) |
| | *Black-out* | |

| *Cue* 22 | To open SCENE 6 | (Page 31) |
| | *Bring up warm interior lighting* | |

EFFECTS PLOT

ACT II

Cue 1   **Digory:** "Polly, don't be a fool!"   (Page 3)
A loud humming noise begins

Cue 2   **Polly:** "It's getting louder."   (Page 3)
Increase humming noise

Cue 3   **Digory:** "Polly, where are you?"   (Page 4)
Humming noise stops

Cue 4   Digory picks up the ring   (Page 5)
A loud humming noise

Cue 5   **Uncle Andrew:** "... the sooner you'll be back."   (Page 5)
Room fills with haze. Humming noise gets very loud.
Echo effect on voice

Cue 6   **Digory:** "One-two-three, jump."   (Page 7)
The rushing sound of a great wind

Cue 7   **Digory:** "You—you girl!" They start to fight   (Page 8)
Bell note gets louder and more menacing, turning into
the crashing sound of falling masonry

Cue 8   **Digory:** "He's the Master Magician."   (Page 9)
The rumble and crash of falling masonry

Cue 9   **Jadis:** "Kabal kalumno."   (Page 9)
Doors crumble to the floor

Cue 10   **Aunt Letitia:** "Well, at least you have some   (Page 13)
manners."
A church bell strikes six

Cue 11   **Digory:** "... but I can hear the sound of galloping."   (Page 13)
Galloping hooves

Cue 12   **Digory:** It's getting very close!"   (Page 13)
Galloping hooves get louder, accompanied by the
sound of whip lashes, panic-stricken neighing, and
then a shattering crash

Cue 13   **Uncle Andrew:** "What happened?"   (Page 13)
More hoofbeats

Cue 14   **Digory:** Go, Polly, go!"   (Page 15)
A monstrous humming

ACT II

Cue 15   **Digory:** "Back to Charn, I hope. Now!"   (Page 16)
Humming noise

MADE AND PRINTED IN GREAT BRITAIN BY
LATIMER TREND & COMPANY LTD PLYMOUTH
MADE IN ENGLAND

CPSIA information can be obtained
at www.ICGtesting.com
Printed in the USA
LVHW081306180820
663418LV00033B/1983

9 780573 150135